INFORMATION MARKETING SIMPLIFIED

"Streamline Your Success in the Digital Age:
A Practical Guide to Information Marketing"

VINCENT SIMS

Copyright ©

Dedication

To those who seek clarity in the realm of information marketing, this book is dedicated to passionate individuals committed to simplifying the complexities, embracing innovation, and transforming knowledge into a powerful force for success. May your journey be illuminated with simplicity and marked by prosperity.

Table of Contents

Acknowledgments

I extend my deepest gratitude to all those who contributed to the creation of this book, "Information Marketing Simplified."

Special thanks to my mentors and industry experts whose insights shaped the content. My appreciation goes to the dedicated team who tirelessly worked on research, editing, and design, bringing this project to life.

To my family and friends, your unwavering support and encouragement fueled my determination. Thank you for being the foundation of my journey.

Lastly, immense gratitude to the readers and learners, whose quest for knowledge inspires the continuous evolution of information marketing. Your curiosity is the driving force behind the simplification of this dynamic field.

Preface

In the age of information overload, navigating the landscape of digital marketing and information dissemination can be overwhelming. "Information Marketing Simplified" emerges as a beacon for those seeking clarity amidst the complexities of this dynamic field.

This book is not just a guide; it's a roadmap designed to demystify the intricacies of information marketing. Drawing on practical insights, real-world examples, and proven strategies, it aims to empower entrepreneurs, marketers, and content creators to harness the power of information in a simplified, yet highly effective, manner.

As the author, my goal is to distill the essence of information marketing, making it accessible to both novices and seasoned professionals. Each chapter unfolds a layer of understanding, leading readers through the evolving landscape of online business, branding, and content monetization.

Whether you're a budding entrepreneur or a seasoned marketer looking to adapt to the ever-changing digital terrain, this book is crafted with you in mind. Prepare to embark on a journey that transforms complexity into clarity and positions you to thrive in the realm of information marketing.

Welcome to "Information Marketing Simplified." Let the journey to digital success begin.

Foreword

Welcome to the world of "Information Marketing Simplified." In the pages that follow, you are about to embark on a transformative journey—a journey that demystifies the complexities of information marketing and unveils a pathway to success marked by strategic simplicity.

In an era where information is abundant, attention spans are fleeting, and digital landscapes are ever-shifting, the need for clarity and focus has never been more critical. This book is not just a guide; it is a compass, navigating you through the intricate terrain of information marketing with a commitment to simplicity at its core.

The journey begins by unraveling the essence of identifying your niche, understanding your audience, and choosing topics that resonate. We delve into the art of crafting compelling content that not only captures attention but fosters genuine connections. Building your brand as an authority within your niche becomes a strategic endeavor, where authenticity and consistency stand as pillars.

As we explore the dynamic realm of strategic marketing and promotion, the spotlight turns to social media—a powerful ally in your quest for audience engagement and brand visibility. The intricacies of email marketing tactics unfold, offering a direct and personalized channel to connect with your audience.

But the true essence of this book lies in the exploration of monetization strategies—strategies that go beyond the conventional, urging you to diversify your income streams and create a resilient business model. In a world where adaptability is key, we unlock the potential for sustainable growth by embracing a multipronged approach to revenue generation.

The simplicity we advocate for is not about oversimplification; it's about distillation—refining the complex into the essential. In these pages, you will find practical insights, actionable strategies, and a roadmap to navigate the intricate yet rewarding landscape of information marketing.

So, whether you are a seasoned marketer seeking to refine your approach or a newcomer eager to make your mark, "Information Marketing Simplified" is your companion on this journey. May you find inspiration, clarity, and a renewed sense of purpose as you navigate the path to success in the world of information marketing.
Get ready to simplify, strategize, and soar.
Best wishes on your journey,

[Vincent Gill]

Chapter 1

Introduction to Information Marketing

- Understanding the Basics

In a world driven by data and digital interactions, information has become a powerful currency. Information marketing, at its core, is the strategic process of transforming knowledge and expertise into valuable products or services. This dynamic field combines elements of marketing, content creation, and entrepreneurship to reach and engage target audiences effectively.

Why Information Marketing Matters:
As businesses and individuals navigate the digital landscape, the ability to share information strategically is a key factor in success. Information marketing provides a structured approach to leverage expertise, build authority, and create valuable content that resonates with a specific audience.

The Core Components:
1. Knowledge Packaging: Information marketing involves packaging your expertise into various forms, such as e-books, online courses, webinars, and more. This allows you to deliver valuable insights to your audience in a digestible format.

2. Target Audience Identification: Understanding your audience is crucial. Information marketing emphasizes the importance of identifying and catering to the specific needs and preferences of your target demographic.

3. Content Distribution: Effectively distributing your content is as important as creating it. Whether through social media, email campaigns, or other channels, information marketing aims to maximize the reach of your valuable insights.

4. Monetization Strategies: Beyond sharing knowledge, information marketing explores ways to monetize expertise. This includes selling information products, offering consulting services, or creating membership programs.

The Evolution of Information Marketing:
Information marketing has evolved with the rise of digital platforms and technological advancements. The accessibility of the internet has democratized information, allowing individuals and businesses of all sizes to participate in the creation and dissemination of valuable content.

Challenges and Opportunities:

While information marketing offers tremendous opportunities, it also presents challenges. Standing out in a crowded digital space, maintaining authenticity, and adapting to ever-changing algorithms are among the hurdles practitioners may face.

As we delve into the intricacies of information marketing in this book, we will explore practical strategies, case studies, and actionable insights to equip you with the knowledge and skills needed to thrive in this exciting and ever-evolving field. Get ready to simplify the complexities and harness the power of information to elevate your digital presence and achieve your goals.

- Key Concepts and Terminology

Navigating the landscape of information marketing requires a solid understanding of key concepts and terminology. Whether you're a novice or a seasoned professional, mastering these fundamental elements is essential for crafting effective strategies and achieving success in this dynamic field.

1. Niche:
   - A niche refers to a specialized segment of the market with its own distinct needs and preferences. In information marketing, identifying and targeting a specific niche allows you to tailor your content and offerings to a more receptive audience.

2. Lead Magnet:

- A lead magnet is a valuable piece of content or incentive offered to potential customers in exchange for their contact information. Common lead magnets include e-books, webinars, and free trials, serving as a gateway to building relationships and nurturing leads.

3. Content Marketing:

- Content marketing involves creating and distributing valuable, relevant, and consistent content to attract and engage a target audience. In information marketing, content is the cornerstone of building authority and establishing trust with your audience.

4. Conversion:

- Conversion refers to the desired action a user takes, such as making a purchase, signing up for a newsletter, or downloading a resource. Understanding conversion metrics is crucial for evaluating the effectiveness of your information marketing efforts.

5. Sales Funnel:
   - A sales funnel represents the stages a potential customer goes through before making a purchase. It typically includes awareness, consideration, and decision stages. Information marketers design funnels to guide prospects through these stages systematically.

6. Evergreen Content:
   - Evergreen content is timeless and retains its relevance over an extended period. Creating evergreen content is a strategic approach in information marketing, ensuring that your materials continue to provide value long after their initial publication.

7. SEO (Search Engine Optimization):
   - SEO involves optimizing your online content to improve its visibility in search

engine results. Information marketers leverage SEO strategies to increase organic traffic to their websites and enhance the discoverability of their content.

8. Monetization:

- Monetization is the process of generating revenue from your information products or services. This can include selling e-books, online courses, consulting services, or implementing affiliate marketing strategies.

9. Call to Action (CTA):

- A call to action is a prompt that encourages users to take a specific action, such as making a purchase, subscribing to a newsletter, or downloading a resource. Effectively crafted CTAs are essential for guiding your audience through the desired conversion paths.

Mastering these key concepts and terminology forms the foundation for a successful information marketing strategy.

As we delve deeper into this book, we will explore how these elements work together to simplify the complexities of information marketing and propel your efforts to new heights.

Chapter 2

Identifying Your Niche

- Market Research Essentials

In the vast landscape of information marketing, finding your niche is a pivotal step toward success. Your niche represents a specialized segment of the market where you can carve out a unique space and cater to a specific audience. Identifying your niche requires a thoughtful approach, blending passion with market demand. Here are the market research essentials to guide you in this crucial process:

1. Understanding Your Interests:

- Start by reflecting on your interests, expertise, and passions. Identify subjects that resonate with you, as enthusiasm for your niche will fuel your commitment and creativity. Consider what topics genuinely captivate your attention and align with your values.

2. Analyzing Market Demand:
- Conduct thorough market research to gauge the demand for potential niches. Look for areas where there is a genuine need or problem that your expertise can address. Tools like keyword research, social media analytics, and industry reports can provide valuable insights into trending topics and audience interests.

3. Defining Your Unique Selling Proposition (USP):
- Clarify what sets you apart within your chosen niche. Your Unique Selling Proposition (USP) should highlight what makes your approach, expertise, or

perspective distinctive. This is a key factor in attracting and retaining your target audience.

4. Assessing Competition:
   - Evaluate the competitive landscape within your identified niche. Analyze existing players, their strengths, and areas where there might be gaps or opportunities. A healthy level of competition can indicate a viable market, but differentiation is crucial for success.

5. Target Audience Profiling:
   - Develop a detailed profile of your ideal audience. Consider demographics, psychographics, and behaviors. Understanding your audience's needs, preferences, and pain points will guide the creation of content that resonates with them.

6. Testing Viability:

- Before fully committing to a niche, test its viability. This can involve creating pilot content, conducting surveys, or running small-scale campaigns to gauge audience response. Use this feedback to refine and adjust your approach as needed.

7. Alignment with Expertise and Passion:
- Ensure that your chosen niche aligns not only with market demand but also with your expertise and passion. The intersection of what you love, what you're good at, and what the market needs is where you'll find the sweet spot for sustainable success.

8. Flexibility for Growth:
- While focusing on a specific niche, allow room for growth and evolution. Industries and trends change, so maintaining flexibility ensures that you can adapt to emerging opportunities and shifting audience interests.

By mastering these market research essentials, you lay the foundation for a successful information marketing journey. Identifying your niche is a strategic decision that aligns your expertise with market demand, setting the stage for impactful content creation and audience engagement.

- Choosing Profitable Topics

In the realm of information marketing, the topics you choose to explore and share play a pivotal role in the success of your endeavors. Strategic content selection involves a thoughtful process that combines market demand, audience interests, and expertise. Here's a guide to help you navigate the art of choosing profitable topics:

1. Market Demand Analysis:
   - Begin by assessing the current market demand for various topics within your niche. Utilize keyword research tools, analyze search trends, and explore social media discussions to identify what topics are capturing the attention of your target audience.

2. Audience Needs and Pain Points:

- Dive deep into understanding the needs and pain points of your target audience. What challenges are they facing? What solutions are they seeking? Choose topics that directly address these concerns, providing valuable insights and practical solutions.

3. Trend Analysis:

- Stay attuned to industry trends and emerging topics. Trends can provide valuable opportunities to create timely and relevant content that resonates with your audience. However, balance trending topics with evergreen content to maintain a timeless appeal.

4. Leverage Your Expertise:

- Capitalize on your own expertise and unique perspective. Choose topics that align with your strengths, experiences, and knowledge. This not only enhances the authenticity of your content but also positions you as an authoritative voice within your niche.

5. Content Variety:

- Diversify your content by exploring a range of topics that cater to different aspects of your niche. This not only keeps your content fresh and engaging but also attracts a broader audience with varying interests within your chosen niche.

6. Addressing Knowledge Gaps:

- Identify gaps in existing content within your niche. If there are topics that are underserved or not thoroughly explored, consider filling these knowledge gaps. Providing comprehensive and in-depth insights on such topics can set you apart as a valuable resource.

7. Align with Audience Feedback:

- Actively seek and incorporate feedback from your audience. Pay attention to comments, questions, and engagement metrics to understand what topics resonate the most. Use this feedback loop to refine your content strategy and consistently meet audience expectations.

8. Monetization Potential:
  - Evaluate the monetization potential of your chosen topics. Consider how each topic aligns with potential revenue streams, such as e-book sales, online courses, consulting services, or affiliate marketing opportunities.

9. Sustainability and Evergreen Appeal:
  - Aim for a balance between trending topics and evergreen content. While trending topics attract immediate attention, evergreen content ensures the longevity of your offerings. Create a content calendar that combines both for sustained impact.

By strategically choosing profitable topics, you position yourself to capture the interest of your audience while building a foundation for sustainable success in information marketing. This thoughtful approach ensures that your content remains relevant, valuable, and aligned with the evolving needs of your audience.

Chapter 3

Creating Compelling Content

- Crafting Engaging Information

In the dynamic world of information marketing, the ability to craft compelling and engaging content is paramount. Your content serves as the bridge connecting your expertise with the needs of your audience. Here's a guide to help you master the art of creating content that captivates and resonates:

1. Understanding Your Audience:
   - Before crafting content, immerse yourself in a deep understanding of your audience.

Know their preferences, pain points, and communication style. Tailor your content to speak directly to their needs, aspirations, and challenges.

2. Clarity and Simplicity:
   - Simplicity is key. Present complex ideas in a clear and accessible manner. Use straightforward language, avoid jargon when unnecessary, and structure your content logically. Make it easy for your audience to grasp and retain the information you're sharing.

3. Storytelling Techniques:
   - Humanize your content through storytelling. Weave narratives that resonate emotionally with your audience. Whether sharing personal experiences, case studies, or success stories, storytelling adds a relatable and memorable dimension to your content.

4. Visual Appeal:

- Leverage the power of visuals to enhance your content. Incorporate images, infographics, and videos to break up text and make your content visually appealing. Visual elements not only grab attention but also aid in conveying complex information more effectively.

5. Interactive Elements:

- Foster engagement through interactive elements. Encourage comments, discussions, and participation from your audience. Incorporate polls, quizzes, and calls to action to create a sense of interactivity and community around your content.

6. Value Proposition:

- Clearly articulate the value your content provides. Whether it's solving a problem, answering a question, or offering insights, communicate the benefits your audience will gain. A strong value proposition encourages continued engagement and builds trust.

7. Consistency in Tone and Style:
   - Establish a consistent tone and style across your content. This creates a recognizable brand voice that resonates with your audience. Whether your tone is informative, conversational, or authoritative, maintain consistency to strengthen your brand identity.

8. Engaging Headlines and Introductions:
   - Capture attention from the start with compelling headlines and introductions. Craft headlines that evoke curiosity and introductions that provide a clear preview of what your content offers. The initial moments are critical in retaining your audience's interest.

9. Mobile-Friendly Design:
   - Optimize your content for mobile viewing. With a growing number of users

accessing content on mobile devices, ensure that your design is responsive and provides a seamless experience across various screen sizes.

10. Call to Action (CTA):

- Conclude your content with a clear call to action. Guide your audience on the next steps, whether it's subscribing to a newsletter, exploring related content, or making a purchase. A well-crafted CTA directs your audience toward meaningful engagement.

As you embark on the journey of crafting engaging information, remember that the heart of compelling content lies in its ability to connect with and inspire your audience. By consistently delivering value and fostering a meaningful connection, you position yourself as a trusted source in the vast landscape of information marketing.

- Multimedia Strategies for Impact

In the fast-paced digital landscape, leveraging multimedia elements is essential to create impactful and engaging content. By incorporating a variety of multimedia formats, you not only capture diverse audience preferences but also enhance the overall effectiveness of your information marketing efforts. Here's a guide to implementing multimedia strategies for maximum impact:

1. Video Content:
    - Explainer Videos: Break down complex concepts using animated or live-action explainer videos. These visually dynamic presentations are excellent for simplifying intricate topics.
    - Webinars and Live Sessions: Engage your audience in real-time through webinars and

live sessions. This format allows for interactive Q&A sessions and fosters a sense of community.

2. Infographics and Visuals:
   - Infographics: Distill information into visually appealing infographics. Condense key points, statistics, or processes into easily digestible graphics for quick comprehension.
   - Data Visualization: Use charts, graphs, and visual representations to convey data. Visualizing information makes it more accessible and memorable for your audience.

3. Podcasts and Audio Content:
   - Podcasts: Dive into auditory storytelling through podcasts. Discuss industry trends, share insights, and interview experts to cater to audiences who prefer consuming content on the go.
   - Audio Guides and Tutorials: Provide step-by-step guides and tutorials in audio

format. This format is convenient for your audience to follow along without needing constant visual attention.

4. Interactive Content:

   - Quizzes and Polls: Integrate interactive quizzes and polls within your content to boost engagement. Encourage your audience to participate and share their opinions, fostering a sense of involvement.

   - Interactive PDFs and eBooks: Create interactive PDFs and eBooks that allow users to navigate, click, and explore additional content within the document.

5. Social Media Engagement:

   - Visual Storytelling on Instagram: Utilize Instagram's visual format for storytelling. Leverage Stories, IGTV, and Reels to share behind-the-scenes content, tips, and updates.

   - Short-Form Videos on TikTok and Reels: Tap into the popularity of short-form videos to deliver quick, entertaining, and informative content.

6. Gamification Elements:
- Gamified Learning Modules: Integrate gamification elements into your content. Create quizzes, challenges, or interactive modules that add an element of fun and competition to the learning experience.

7. Virtual and Augmented Reality (VR/AR):
- Virtual Tours: Offer virtual tours or experiences related to your niche. This immersive approach is particularly effective for industries such as travel, real estate, or hands-on tutorials.
- AR Product Demonstrations: Use augmented reality for product demonstrations. Allow users to visualize products in their own space, enhancing their understanding and decision-making process.

8. Collaborations and Influencer Partnerships:

- Guest Collaborations: Collaborate with influencers, experts, or complementary brands for joint content creation. This not only expands your reach but also adds diverse perspectives to your multimedia content.

By strategically implementing these multimedia strategies, you can cater to diverse learning preferences and create a more immersive and impactful information marketing experience. Remember, the key is to align your chosen formats with your content goals and the preferences of your target audience.

Chapter 4

Building Your Brand

- Establishing Authority in Your Niche

In the competitive landscape of information marketing, building a strong brand is not just about creating a recognizable logo; it's about establishing authority within your niche. Your brand should be synonymous with expertise, trustworthiness, and value. Here's a guide to help you navigate the process of building your brand and positioning yourself as an authoritative figure:

1. Define Your Brand Identity:

- Clearly define your brand identity, including your mission, values, and unique selling proposition (USP). Your brand identity forms the foundation for how you present yourself to your audience.

2. Consistent Visual Branding:
- Maintain consistent visual elements across all platforms. This includes your logo, color scheme, typography, and imagery. Consistency fosters recognition and reinforces your brand identity.

3. Craft a Compelling Brand Story:
- Share your journey and expertise through a compelling brand story. Communicate why you are passionate about your niche and how your experiences uniquely position you as an authority.

4. Quality Content Creation:
- Consistently produce high-quality, valuable content. Whether it's blog posts, videos, or podcasts, each piece of content

should reflect your expertise and provide meaningful insights to your audience.

5. Engage Authentically:
   - Engage with your audience authentically. Respond to comments, participate in discussions, and showcase the personality behind your brand. Authenticity builds trust, a crucial component of authority.

6. Leverage Social Proof:
   - Showcase testimonials, case studies, and positive feedback from satisfied clients or customers. Social proof is a powerful tool for establishing credibility and reinforcing your authority in the eyes of your audience.

7. Expert Positioning through Thought Leadership:
   - Position yourself as a thought leader within your niche. Share in-depth analyses, industry trends, and forward-thinking insights. Contribute to discussions and

forums, showcasing your expertise and staying ahead of the curve.

8. Publish Authoritative Content:
- Create cornerstone content that establishes your authority. This could be comprehensive guides, whitepapers, or research studies that delve deep into topics relevant to your niche.

9. Collaborate with Influencers and Peers:
- Collaborate with influencers or respected figures in your niche. Partnerships and collaborations can amplify your reach and lend credibility to your brand.

10. Offer Value Beyond Products:
- Beyond promoting your products or services, provide value to your audience through free resources, educational content, or community building. This approach fosters a sense of reciprocity and positions your brand as genuinely invested in the success of your audience.

11. Attend and Speak at Industry Events:
   - Participate in industry conferences, webinars, and events. Speaking engagements and panel discussions are excellent opportunities to showcase your expertise and connect with a broader audience.

12. Build a Community:
   - Create a community around your brand. Whether it's through a forum, social media group, or other platforms, a community fosters a sense of belonging and loyalty among your audience.

By implementing these strategies consistently, you can build a brand that not only stands out but also holds a position of authority in your niche. Remember, authority is earned through a combination of expertise, trust, and a genuine commitment to delivering value to your audience.

- Effective Branding Techniques

Branding is more than just a logo; it's the soul of your business, the essence that resonates with your audience. Effective branding techniques go beyond aesthetics; they create a lasting impression and cultivate a connection between your brand and your customers. Here's a guide to help you employ techniques that will elevate your brand and make it memorable:

1. Define Your Brand Strategy:
   - Start with a clear brand strategy that outlines your mission, values, and unique selling proposition (USP). Understanding who you are and what you stand for is the foundation of effective branding.

2. Create a Distinctive Logo:
   - Design a memorable and versatile logo. Your logo should be simple, scalable, and reflective of your brand identity. Ensure it works well across various platforms and maintains clarity in different sizes.

3. Consistent Visual Elements:
   - Establish a consistent visual identity. This includes color schemes, fonts, and imagery. Consistency builds recognition and helps your audience associate specific visuals with your brand.

4. Develop a Unique Tone of Voice:
   - Craft a distinctive tone of voice that aligns with your brand personality. Whether it's friendly, professional, or humorous, your tone should be consistent across all communication channels.

5. Emphasize Brand Values:

- Communicate your brand values authentically. Clearly express what your brand stands for and how it aligns with the values of your target audience. Consumers are increasingly drawn to brands with a sense of purpose.

6. Storytelling Through Brand Narrative:
- Tell a compelling brand story. Highlight your journey, challenges overcome, and milestones achieved. A well-crafted narrative adds depth and emotional connection to your brand.

7. Personalize Customer Interactions:
- Personalize customer interactions. From emails to social media responses, inject a personal touch that reflects the human side of your brand. Personalization fosters a sense of connection and loyalty.

8. Consistent Branding Across Platforms:
- Ensure consistency across all platforms. From your website to social media profiles,

your branding should be seamless. A unified brand presence reinforces credibility and professionalism.

9. Engage in Social Media Branding:
   - Leverage social media platforms strategically for brand building. Showcase your brand personality through posts, visuals, and engagement. Social media is a powerful tool for creating a dynamic brand persona.

10. Implement Brand Guidelines:
    - Develop comprehensive brand guidelines. These guidelines should cover logo usage, color codes, typography, and overall design principles. Consistent application of guidelines maintains a cohesive brand image.

11. Deliver a Consistent Customer Experience:
    - Ensure a consistent customer experience at every touchpoint. From the first

interaction to post-purchase support, align your customer experience with the promises and values of your brand.

12. Monitor and Evolve:
- Regularly assess your brand's performance and audience perceptions. Embrace evolution when needed, keeping your brand relevant and aligned with changing market dynamics.

By incorporating these effective branding techniques, you not only create a strong visual identity but also build a brand that resonates with your audience on a deeper level. Remember, successful branding is an ongoing process that evolves with your business and the needs of your customers.

Chapter 5.

Strategic Marketing and Promotion

- Leveraging Social Media

In the digital age, social media has emerged as a powerhouse for strategic marketing and promotion. With billions of active users, platforms like Facebook, Instagram, Twitter, LinkedIn, and others offer unparalleled opportunities to connect with your audience, build brand awareness, and drive engagement. Here's a guide on leveraging social media as a crucial component of your strategic marketing and promotion efforts:

1. Know Your Audience:
   - Start by understanding your target audience. Different social media platforms attract distinct demographics. Tailor your

content and engagement strategies to align with the preferences and behaviors of your specific audience.

2. Choose the Right Platforms:
    - Not all social media platforms are created equal. Select platforms that align with your brand and where your audience is most active. For instance, visual content may perform well on Instagram, while professional content finds its place on LinkedIn.

3. Develop a Content Calendar:
    - Create a content calendar to ensure a consistent and cohesive social media presence. Plan and schedule your posts in advance, considering key events, trends, and your overall marketing strategy.

4. Visual Storytelling:
    - Harness the power of visual storytelling. Use compelling visuals, including images, infographics, and videos, to convey your

brand message. Visual content tends to grab attention and is more likely to be shared.

5. Engage and Interact:
   - Social media is a two-way street. Actively engage with your audience by responding to comments, asking questions, and participating in conversations. Interaction builds a sense of community and strengthens your brand relationship.

6. Utilize Paid Advertising:
   - Leverage paid advertising options on social media platforms. Targeted ads allow you to reach specific demographics, ensuring that your content reaches the most relevant audience for your brand.

7. Run Contests and Giveaways:
   - Encourage engagement through contests and giveaways. This not only boosts participation but also expands your brand's reach as participants share your content with their networks.

8. Collaborate with Influencers:
- Partner with influencers in your niche. Influencers already have established audiences, and their endorsement can significantly amplify your brand visibility and credibility.

9. Monitor Analytics and Metrics:
- Regularly analyze social media analytics to understand the performance of your content. Track metrics such as engagement, reach, and conversions. Use these insights to refine your strategy over time.

10. Utilize Hashtags Strategically:
- Incorporate relevant hashtags to increase the discoverability of your content. Research trending and industry-specific hashtags to join larger conversations and expand your brand's visibility.

11. Live Video and Stories:

- Embrace live video features and stories for real-time interaction. Live content provides an authentic and immediate connection with your audience, fostering a sense of urgency and exclusivity.

12. Cross-Promote Across Platforms:
- Cross-promote your content across different social media platforms. Share snippets, teasers, or adapted content to reach a broader audience and maintain a consistent brand message.

Social media is a dynamic and ever-evolving landscape. By strategically incorporating these techniques, you can maximize the impact of your marketing and promotion efforts, building a strong and engaged online community around your brand. Remember, the key is to be authentic, consistent, and adaptive to the evolving trends in the social media space.

- Email Marketing Tactics

Email marketing remains a cornerstone of digital communication, offering a direct and personalized channel to connect with your audience. When executed strategically, email campaigns can drive engagement, nurture leads, and contribute significantly to the overall success of your marketing efforts. Here's a guide to employing effective email marketing tactics:

1. Build a Quality Email List:
   - Prioritize quality over quantity when building your email list. Obtain explicit consent for communication, segment your audience based on preferences, and regularly clean and update your list to ensure relevance.

2. Personalization for Engagement:

- Personalize your emails to resonate with individual recipients. Address them by name, tailor content based on their preferences, and use segmentation to send targeted messages. Personalization enhances engagement and fosters a stronger connection.

3. Engaging Subject Lines:
    - Craft compelling subject lines that captivate attention. The subject line is the first interaction users have with your email, and a well-crafted one encourages higher open rates.

4. Clear Call to Action (CTA):
    - Clearly define the action you want recipients to take. Whether it's making a purchase, downloading a resource, or signing up for an event, a concise and compelling CTA guides your audience toward the desired outcome.

5. Mobile Optimization:

- Optimize your emails for mobile devices. With a significant portion of users accessing emails on mobile devices, responsive design ensures a seamless and engaging experience across various screen sizes.

6. A/B Testing:
- Experiment with A/B testing to refine your strategies. Test variations of subject lines, content, visuals, and CTAs to identify what resonates best with your audience. Use data-driven insights to optimize future campaigns.

7. Value-Driven Content:
- Provide valuable content that addresses the needs and interests of your audience. Whether it's educational content, exclusive offers, or relevant updates, delivering value keeps subscribers engaged.

8. Automated Workflows:
- Implement automated workflows to streamline communication. Set up drip

campaigns, welcome sequences, and personalized nurture tracks based on user behaviors. Automation ensures timely and relevant interactions.

9. Segment Your Audience:
    - Segment your email list based on demographics, behaviors, or engagement levels. Targeted communication tailored to specific segments increases relevance and engagement.

10. Social Proof and Testimonials:
    - Include social proof and testimonials in your emails. Positive reviews, testimonials, or user-generated content build trust and credibility, influencing purchasing decisions.

11. Personalized Recommendations:
    - Utilize data to offer personalized product or content recommendations. Analyze past interactions and behaviors to suggest items

or topics aligned with individual preferences.

12. Measure and Analyze Results:
- Regularly measure the performance of your email campaigns. Analyze open rates, click-through rates, conversion rates, and other relevant metrics. Use this data to refine your approach and enhance future campaigns.

Effective email marketing is a dynamic blend of creativity, data-driven insights, and strategic planning. By incorporating these tactics into your campaigns, you can cultivate a strong and engaged email subscriber base, driving meaningful interactions and contributing to your overall marketing success.

Chapter 6

Monetization Strategies

- Diversifying Income Streams

In the ever-evolving landscape of information marketing, diversifying income streams is a key strategy to ensure long-term sustainability and growth. Relying on a single source of revenue can be limiting, and diversification opens up opportunities to reach new audiences and adapt to changing market dynamics. Here's a guide on implementing effective monetization strategies by diversifying your income streams:

1. Digital Products and E-Books:

- Create and sell digital products, such as e-books, guides, templates, or printables. These products can cater to specific niches within your audience, providing valuable insights or solutions in a convenient and easily accessible format.

2. Online Courses and Training Programs:
   - Develop and sell online courses and training programs. Leverage your expertise to offer in-depth, structured learning experiences. Platforms like Udemy, Teachable, or your website can serve as hubs for hosting and selling these courses.

3. Membership Programs and Subscription Models:
   - Establish membership programs or subscription models that offer exclusive content, community access, or premium features to paying members. Recurring revenue from subscriptions provides a stable income stream.

4. Consulting and Coaching Services:

- Monetize your expertise through consulting or coaching services. Offer one-on-one or group sessions to clients seeking personalized guidance. This human-centric approach can be a lucrative income stream.

5. Affiliate Marketing:

- Engage in affiliate marketing by promoting products or services relevant to your niche. Earn a commission for each sale or lead generated through your unique affiliate links. Select partners that align with your brand and audience.

6. Sponsored Content and Partnerships:

- Collaborate with brands for sponsored content or partnerships. This can involve featuring products or services in your content, hosting sponsored events, or co-creating valuable resources. Sponsored collaborations diversify revenue while expanding your reach.

7. Ad Revenue and Sponsorships:

- Monetize your platform through ad revenue and sponsorships. If you have a blog, podcast, or YouTube channel with a significant following, advertisers may pay to feature their content or products to your audience.

8. Physical Products and Merchandise:

- Explore the creation and sale of physical products or merchandise. Branded items such as apparel, accessories, or even specialized tools can serve as additional revenue streams while strengthening brand recognition.

9. Event Hosting and Workshops:

- Host live or virtual events, workshops, or master classes. Charge participants for access to your expertise and exclusive content. Events not only generate revenue but also foster a sense of community.

10. Licensing and Syndication:

- License your content for syndication or reuse. This can include selling the rights to repurpose your articles, videos, or other content to third parties. Licensing provides a passive income stream.

11. Crowdfunding and Donations:

- Engage your audience through crowdfunding platforms or donation models. Platforms like Patreon allow your audience to support you directly in exchange for exclusive perks, content, or early access.

12. E-commerce and Dropshipping:

- Venture into e-commerce by selling physical products directly to your audience. Consider dropshipping as a low-risk option, where you fulfill orders through a third-party supplier.

By diversifying your income streams, you not only enhance your financial stability but also create a resilient business model that can adapt to market changes. The key is to align your monetization strategies with your brand, audience, and the value you provide, ensuring a harmonious and sustainable revenue mix.

- Maximizing Revenue from Information Products

Maximizing revenue from information products involves strategic planning, effective marketing, and delivering high-value content. Here are key strategies to achieve success in this endeavor:

1. Identify a Niche Market:
   - Target a specific audience with a genuine need for the information you provide.
   - Conduct market research to understand your audience's pain points and preferences.

2. Create High-Quality Content:
   - Develop information products that are well-researched, comprehensive, and solve real problems.
   - Invest in professional design and presentation to enhance perceived value.

3. Implement Tiered Pricing:
   - Offer different product packages at varying price points to cater to a diverse customer base.
   - Include premium options with additional features or personalized support for higher prices.

4. Build a Sales Funnel:
   - Create a sales funnel to guide potential customers from awareness to purchase.
   - Utilize free content, lead magnets, and email campaigns to nurture leads and convert them into buyers.

5. Leverage Multiple Distribution Channels:
   - Sell your information products through various channels, such as your website, online marketplaces, and affiliate networks.
   - Explore partnerships with influencers or other businesses to expand your reach.

6. Implement Upsells and Cross-Sells:

- Offer complementary products or upgrades to customers during the checkout process.
- Increase the average transaction value by suggesting related items or premium versions.

7. Optimize for Repeat Sales:
  - Foster customer loyalty by providing ongoing value, such as regular updates or exclusive content.
  - Implement subscription models or membership programs to encourage recurring revenue.

8. Utilize Effective Marketing:
  - Employ content marketing, social media, and search engine optimization to increase visibility.
  - Leverage testimonials, case studies, and success stories to build credibility and trust.

9. Invest in Customer Support:

- Provide excellent customer support to enhance the overall customer experience.

- Address customer inquiries promptly and offer assistance to build a positive reputation.

10. Monitor and Analyze Data:

- Use analytics tools to track sales, customer behavior, and marketing performance.

- Adjust strategies based on data insights to continually optimize your revenue generation.

By implementing these strategies, you can create a robust framework for maximizing revenue from information products, ensuring long-term success in a competitive market.

Conclusion

As we reach the conclusion of "Information Marketing Simplified," the journey through the intricacies of this dynamic field leaves us with a clear understanding: simplicity is the cornerstone of success. In a landscape marked by constant evolution and diverse opportunities, simplifying the complexities of information marketing is not about oversimplification; it's about strategic clarity.

We've explored the fundamentals, from identifying your niche and choosing profitable topics to crafting compelling content and building a brand that resonates. The strategic marketing tactics, leveraging social media, and diversifying income streams showcased the multifaceted nature of a successful information marketing approach.

This book is more than a guide; it's a roadmap to unlocking the full potential of your expertise and connecting with an audience hungry for valuable insights. We've emphasized the importance of authenticity, engagement, and providing genuine value to your audience—principles that transcend trends and withstand the test of time.

As you embark on your information marketing journey, remember that simplicity doesn't mean sacrificing depth or impact. It's about streamlining your efforts, focusing on what truly matters, and adapting to the evolving needs of your audience. Your success lies not just in mastering the strategies outlined in these pages but in the ongoing commitment to growth, learning, and staying attuned to the pulse of your niche.

In this simplified approach, you hold the power to transform information into influence, and influence into a thriving, sustainable business. May your endeavors be marked by innovation, resilience, and a passion for sharing knowledge. As you apply the principles unveiled in this book, may you find fulfillment in the impact you create and the community you nurture.

Here's to your continued success in the simplified yet dynamic world of information marketing. May your journey be marked by clarity, purpose, and the unwavering pursuit of excellence.

Information Marketing Simplified

Information Marketing Simplified